BUSINESS PLAN

Best Proven Techniques to Writing a
Successful Business Plan to Maximize a
Profitable Business

CONTENTS

INTRODUCTION

I want to thank you for purchasing this book, "Business Plan Writing: Best proven techniques to writing a successful business plan to maximize a profitable business" and hope it helps you in your entrepreneurial journey.

A business plan is nothing but a detailed written account of your future business or maybe current business. This document describes the entire work plan that you ought to do in order to run your business in a strategic manner one step at a time.

The objective of a business plan is to explain and decipher your business idea and fragment it into the most minute detail. It also explains, questions like (that might be in your head) - Why is your business project required in the market, how will it succeed and who will take this responsibility to make it happen.

The purpose of this book is to leave with the following:

- An understanding to define business planning.
- Ability to list down the objectives of the plan
- The most appropriate uses of the plan
- Define the target audience
- Develop the understanding of extending these objectives to external and internal audience accordingly
- Elaborate on the key components of the business plan
- Steps to be taken in order to lay out the business planning process
- Build effective business plan

In the twenty - first it is necessary and important to have a business plan. The need for an effective business plan has never been so apparent and critical. The world around is competitive and is moving at an accelerating rate with a consistent demanding pressure scenario.

Today's economic reality is faced with new and gut wrenching challenges; hence, making a business plan cannot just remain a regular exercise. It has to be detailed, precise and should have a competitive advantage. Planning must lay the foundation for a sustainable business establishment and must cover all the aspects of an effective plan of action. The book also helps you understand how to create a business plan for startup which can also be implemented for any other company.

I want to thank you for downloading this eBook once again and hope you like it.

CHAPTER 1

WHAT CHARACTERIZES A BUSINESS PLAN?

A business plan, as the name suggests, is a plan that helps in setting up a business and carrying it forward. It also takes into account the allocation of resources and focuses on the essentials required for the business to be successful. It also includes a contingency plan in order to tackle problems. Business plans have been implemented for quite some time now and are extremely helpful in setting up your own business.

Business plans must also include monetary clauses: the source of funds initially, loans, etc. Business plans will prove to be immensely helpful in optimizing the business and will aid in accomplishing the desired result.

What is a Start - up plan?

Start-up plans are very basic plans which include the mission statement, a summary, the essentials required for success, market and break-even analyses. Such a plan gives a good idea as to whether or not to pursue the idea. It also tells you if there is a scope for the idea to be a big success. However, businesses cannot run on the basis of such plans.

What does a standard business plan consist of?

A business plan that is devised on the basis of advice received from business experts has a certain set of standard elements. The plan format and shape may vary, but every business plan must contain certain components for it is classified as a standard business plan.

Company descriptions, management and financial analyses and market forecasts are some of these components.

The structure of your plan depends on what you want to use it for. If you are making it for internal purposes only, you need not include information like background details and description of your management team because you are already aware of such details. However, if you are sending the plan out to banks and other potential investors, you need to include those details so that they can have a better idea of your business. Make your plan in accordance with its purpose.

What is most important about a business plan?

The answer to this question depends on what the purpose of the business plan. More often than not, the most important part is the cash flow analysis and details regarding specific implementations.

- Cash flow is extremely vital to a company and it is not very easy to keep a track of it. Profits do not necessarily guarantee cash in the bank. It is a common misconception which should be avoided. Due to this misconception, many companies get shut down even though they are profitable.

- Implementation details are also important because they are the building blocks of your business. Every strategy or every idea that you come up with may look good on paper. For them to be materialized, proper implementation plans are necessary. No matter how brilliant your idea may be; if its implementation is done incorrectly, the efficiency goes down.

Standard blueprint of a business plan

As mentioned above, there are certain components that are essential for every business plan. For instance, business plans generally start with what is called an EXECUTIVE Summary.

BUSINESS PLAN

The order in which the main components feature in your plan doesn't really matter but the recommended order is as follows:

1. Executive Summary: This includes about a page of highlights of your plan. It is advisable to write this at the end. (Place it at the head of the plan)

2. Company Description: This takes into account the start-up plan, legal establishments and other details.

3. Product or Service: Describe your product here. Emphasize on how it would benefit the customer.

4. Market Analysis: Similar to what the name suggests, this section contains your analysis of the market and other details such as customer needs and how you aim to satisfy them.

5. Strategy and Implementation: Include your strategies and ideas. Describe them in detail. Also include how you choose to implement the above mentioned ideas.

6. Management Team: Enlist each of the members of your management team. This is important information as far as investors are concerned.

7. Financial Analysis: This is another important part of the plan. You need to mention your projected profit and cash flow table.

CHAPTER 2

ALL THAT MATTERS IS THE FINAL RESULT

Assume that you are a consultant who is writing a business plan for your company. You come across a Professor from your business school whose class you attended a few years ago. You have made quite a few successful business plans, but not all of them worked for your company or any other company you were a consultant for. You might have helped increase the sales of a company and in turn increased their turnover helping them break even earlier!

During the discussion, your business professor asks you 'What is the value of the business plan that you create?' You might think for a very long time but what is the first thought that you get? That it is worth close to a thousand pounds! That is what you tell your professor. But your professor says that you have got it all wrong, so wrong! You are shocked are you not?

That is where you are wrong. Your plan is worthy only if it helps influencing the decisions that you are making for your company and the money you have in your bank account because of this decision. You might not believe this now, but it is the truth. You must remember this vital lesson while creating future plans.

You have to use this idea while creating any plan for your company. Your plans are always measured by the results they show. It could be a plan that has been written beautifully, but the result of your business is what matters most!

What does a plan need to be called "good"?

The most ideal way to judge a plan is on the basis of its contents. By looking at the value of its contents, you can categorize a plan as good or bad. Certain qualities can make a plan more likely to attain good results and these are extremely important. As mentioned above, even if the plan is devised excellently, if the implementation is not appropriate, the plan fails. Hence, even the implementation is important to categorize a plan as good or bad.

A business plan also depends on the human elements and effort put in the implementation process. Following up a plan with appropriate implementation is vital for the plan to be a success. Tracking your progress is another key element to the success of a plan. These points will be tackled with later on in the book. For now, let us look at what makes a plan itself good or bad.

You need a good plan to even have a chance of successful implementation. There are certain elements that a plan must have to be good. Ask yourself the following questions while making your plan in order to devise it properly.

1. Is the plan straightforward? Will the implementation process be easy? It is better to have a simple, straightforward plan rather than a complex plan which is hard for people to understand.

2. Is the plan specific? It is a good practice to have a specific business plan. A plan without any particular people or actions required and one without a fixed date of completion will rarely ever be successful. More than anything, it is extremely important to have a date of completion.

3. Another essential quality that a plan must have is that it needs to be realistic. A plan with outlandish goals will not only be near impossible to implement, but will also affect the morale of the people involved. They will be

aware of the uphill task that they are up against and this will end up demotivating them.

4. Finally, once you have devised your plan, you need to ask yourself if it is complete and if it includes all the elements needed. It is true that the elements of plans vary with the purpose, but the main base elements common to every plan need to be present.

Uses and advantages of a business plan

Devising a plan becomes helpful when you are trying to complete a task. This is because it helps you organize yourself and this aids in completing the task easily. Same is the case with a business; having a plan will increase the chances of completion. Aimlessly working towards a goal is less preferable when compared to working towards it in an organized fashion.

- Fix your objectives and goals and also decide how you want to implement them.

- Have regular business reviews to track your progress.

- Define a new business.

- Apply for a loan.

- Make sure your partners get along well with each other and that there is no bad blood between them.

- Place a price on your business in the event of sale.

- Look to expand your boundaries and explore different avenues for project ventures.

Never think that there isn't enough time to devise a plan

Far too many businessmen make business plans as and when required. For instance, when a banker or an investor requests for a plan, one is made right from scratch and submitted. This is a wrong practice. It is always good to have a plan even though it takes time to devise one. Business plans help in achieving the goal easier.

What not to do with a business plan

- The first thing to keep in mind is to avoid showing off. Nobody wants to know how familiar a subject business is to you.

- Keep your business plan short and sweet. Nobody is willing to read a long business plan. Your business plan should be a maximum of 50 pages only! Submitting long plans will also affect your chances of landing investors because they wouldn't want to read the entire plan.

CHAPTER 3

WHAT ARE BUSINESS PLAN OBJECTIVES?

For any successful business management it is extremely essential that you have a great business plan. The unforeseen events, new competitors, plausible market scenarios that might enter at some point must also be mentioned. Business planning objectives must include risk factors, marketing strategies, how the business will run and most importantly how these objectives would be measured.

Objectives are the heart and soul of any business plan. They are laid down to give clarity to the current status of a business and the future it is heading to. In order to put it simply, objectives are like your checklist, you can keep a track of your work, business growth, etc. with the help of these objectives.

 Well – chosen goals and objectives will lead a business project in the right direction (especially in the case of start - ups) and an established company in the right exponential growth.

The objectives should be **SMART:**

- Specific
- Measurable
- Achievable
- Realistic
- Time - oriented

Specific

A vague objective leads to poor results and an unclear strategy. Questions like, what needs to be done? "How will it be done?" are described in a specific objective. The end results will yield the work that needs to be done. The way this objective is written, it actually appears absolutely feasible for anyone to understand and extremely easy to interpret. When anyone hears about your specific goal they know exactly what you are aiming for, that's how specific your objective should be.

Measurable

When you have measurable objectives, then it allows you to keep a track of your progress or the anticipations around it. When making a business plan you need to understand and be aware about the steps that you will need to take that will lead you to your desired expectations. Assessment scales like quantity, quality etc., define the measurable parameters for any business plan.

Achievable

Attainable and achievable! Objectives must be laid down in a way that they are attainable and are achievable. Questions like –"can this be achieved? "Can we do it?" are answered when a target is assessed on this parameter. It basically weighs all the available resources, timeline, capacity and the experience to fulfill the desired vision.

Realistic

Based on the resources, it is important to keep the objectives realistic. However, it does not imply that one should not be ambitious but it is highly important to be aware of your strengths and weaknesses.

Time bound

The only way to keep a track on the progress of work is to define a timeline to those tasks. Time oriented objectives provide a start and end date to any task. This is just the simplest way to put it. Other than this, all the milestones or checkpoints can be traced easily once a timeline is assigned to it. It also helps to make any necessary modification to the work progress plan whenever required.

CHAPTER 4

DIFFERENTIATION - GOALS AND OBJECTIVES

Many a times we use the terms "goals" and "objectives" interchangeably, especially when building a business plan. However, it is really important to know the distinction between the two and use them effectively to create a very solid and polished business plan. There needs to be an understanding of the differences between a goal and an objective. Avoid confusion when formulating a business plan and clearly establish the disparity between the goals and objectives.

Goals

Goals represent your aspirations, dreams and expectation. These statements are made to declare and clearly state the future of your business project. In order to provide a direction and clarity to your business project, it is important that you complete the exercise of goal setting.

Not only should that, your goals have to go hand in hand with the aspirations and values of your business. The language used in goals need not be very formal. Goals also allow you to explore your mind space and think conceptually and not get stopped or trapped in creative analysis.

What are objectives?

In order to achieve goals certain steps need to be taken, these definite and necessary steps are called objectives. They are straight, formal and without any emotion. They are essentially measurable and quantifiable. Also realistic and time bound.

Objectives are used to measure the success and progress towards the set goals. Without setting up the objectives, goals seem rather impossible to achieve. Meeting of objectives is motivational as it shows the ladder that one is climbing towards achieving the set goals, thus providing a sense of accomplishment.

Summary

- Goals and objectives are both tools for accomplishing what you want to achieve.

- Goals are mostly long term, whereas objectives are usually short or medium term.

- Goals shouldn't be measured; on the other hand the success of the objective should be measured easily.

- Goals are hard to quantify or tie in a timeline, but the objectives have a definite timeline and are quantifiable.

CHAPTER 5

COMPONENTS OF A BUSINESS PLAN

Writing a business plan is no mean feat. In order to make an effective business plan one needs to make sure not to forget the essential components of a business plan. Come back to this list and make sure your plan includes the following components.

Executive Summary

This 1 to 1.5 page summary is the synopsis of your entire business plan. This summary provides an overview of the whole business project. It is one of the most critical aspects of any business plan. This summary tells the reader exactly what the business plan is all about, and clearly states the outline of the business plan. Executive summary captures the vision, mission, values and the opportunity of your business project plans to seize.

Market Analysis

A refined description of market analysis shows the depth of your understanding of the industry that you are a part of or are venturing into. A very important research that will only boost your confidence, it is a must. A market analysis enables you to become familiar with the current trends of the market. This analysis prepares you to position your business plan most appropriately and identify potential stakeholders. It also helps in formulating a suitable marketing strategy.

It also gives an indication of the scope of growth that will help envisioning the future growth of your business plan. A marketing analysis provides the backbone to survive in this competitive environment

Company Description

This section includes a deeper understanding of all the different elements of your business plan. The company description includes all the factors that will make your business planning process effective and it also provides comprehensive information on the nature of your business.

Organization and Management

This self – explanatory component includes the structure of the organization, details about the ownership of the company and the description of the team that manages the company. Also included here is the detailed information about the panel and the board of directors.

Marketing and Sales Strategies

A good marketing strategy creates customers. Customers generate sales. This is the life source of any business plan. Along with a marketing strategy, this section also includes tactics that will help you achieve the set targets of your company.

Product Line

This is your chance to prove yourself as the most sought after business proposition. This section is where you describe the kind of service and unique product that you would provide in the market. It is highly critical to emphasize on the benefits that your business plan will provide and also the reasons why your product or service is better than the rest.

Funding Requirements

Here you describe the funds that you would require in order to start or expand your business.

Financial Requirement

Develop and showcase at least 2 to 3 years of financial strategy. Such a strategy is developed by analyzing the market and setting clear objectives. A good business plan is a constant exercise that has to be performed again and again. A good business plan is ever evolving. It has to be visited often based on the changing external scenarios, exceeded expectations and some failed assumptions. Set a process and a structure may be monthly or quarterly where you make sure that you visit your financial plan. It is good to have a mentor by your side or at least an experienced team member.

S.W.O.T Analysis

The main purpose of this analysis is to strengthen your strategic understanding in analyzing all the aspects involved in business planning. SWOT analysis helps you to analyze things that you might have not otherwise even thought about. Things that will help you inspect your business plan to minutest of details.

Strength (Existing potential)

They describe the positive factors that would work in your favor which are already present within your company or organization. These factors could be tangible or intangible. When listing down your strengths, ask the following questions:

- What kind of resources and how many do you have?
  - It could be the knowledge of the people in your team, their experience, capacity, skills, education, credentials etc.

- What do you know and how well you know it?

Tangible assets of the company are critical and it is important to list them down. Some of the tangible factors are - existing customer database, technology, capital etc.

- How is your research and development capacity?
- What potential do you have to offer to the current competitive market?
- What are you advantages over your competitors?

Weaknesses

To know weaknesses is as important as knowing your strengths. In a business set – up weaknesses play at a disadvantage that stops you from achieving your goals and objectives. In order to level the competitive market, it is important that you fine tune these areas and up your game. When jotting down your weaknesses, ask yourself the following questions:

- What factors are well within your control that needs attention?
- Which factors will stop you from gaining competitive edge?
- Which areas need immediate attention and refinement?
- What are the things that you do not have - it could be human resource, expertise in a specific skill.

Opportunity

These are options that are available or to be recognized (eventually) that are going to add immense value to the existing system and lead your business project in a way that it prospers and succeeds. When identifying opportunities ask yourself the following questions:

- What opportunities exist in your market?
- What is the current scenario of the external environment that can prove beneficial to you?
- How is the perception of your business?

- Are there are any current market shifts that can create unique and innovative opportunities?

Threats (external, negative factors)

There is nothing you can do about threats. This is something which is not in your control, but having contingency plans do help mitigate the situation in the most appropriate fashion. When pointing out threats, ask yourself the following questions:

- Who are your potential competitors?
- What are some of those factors that could pose a threat to your business?
- What are the most plausible circumstances that can jeopardize your marketing efforts?
- What have been some of the uncharted changes in the market scenario?
- What are the shifts in government policy or any other significant aspect?
- Has there been a recent product in the market that might make your product vulnerable and less interesting?

CHAPTER 6

MINI PLANNING - BREAK DOWN AND ASSESS

At any point of your business plans take time to stop and assess it. You must do this at the start obviously in order to know if the plan might be a success or not. As your business plan progresses, stop at regular intervals and check how it has come along so far, how much is left and whether or not you will be able to finish it by the due date. At the beginning, assess your objectives, the aim of the plan and what are the elements required to achieve success.

Objectives

You will have to set all your objectives at the beginning of the business plan. Sales objectives, market share objectives and projected profit are some of the essentials that need to be stated in your plan.

You have to be specific in stating your objectives. For instance, when you mention your projected profits you need to give a certain number or range (small range). Do not use vague terms such as "we want to be the best" or "the business will grow rapidly if..." Another thing to keep in mind is that whatever numbers you state or goals you set make sure that they are rational and achievable.

Your goals or objectives need to be measurable. Stating things like you will be the best or you will maximize customer satisfaction are words that cannot be measured. This does not really appeal to many investors or bankers for that matter. So make sure that you have concrete, specific and practical goals mentioned in your plan.

Your goals could be tangible or intangible. It is best to ensure that your goals are tangible meaning you can see yourself achieving those goals! If you find that you are unable to plan these tangible goals, try to identify a way to measure them. For instance, if you know that the brand and the awareness are vital aspects for your company, identify ways to measure the growth in the awareness and branding of your company. It could be done through schedules and questionnaires which will help you identify the perfect solution to the problem. You can set goals for every aspect of your company – growth in the market, market shares, and equity shares and also measure the actual market share. You can always focus on the satisfaction of your customers – see if you can identify ways to satisfy your customers with the existing products and services that you are providing.

Aim of the business plan

This is also referred to as the mission statement of a company. Mission statements are used primarily to explain your business concept. Mission statements generally include what the main goal is. It also throws light on what market you will be contributing to and how you think your product will bring about customer satisfaction.

What market do you contribute to?

This is extremely vital to be mentioned in your plan. Think of all the types of businesses you could be a part of. Do not miss out on anything as the greater the number of markets that will benefit from your idea, the greater are the chances of landing investors. Forgetting to mention these markets can affect your company adversely. One such example is the railroads. At the time, they thought they were only in the business of running trains on tracks. Little did they know how important the transport of goods would become.

Customer Satisfaction

How your product will bring about customer satisfaction is something that needs to be mentioned in your mission statement as well. The importance of this cannot be overstated. When potential investors are reading your business plan, this portion can really sway them. If you can explain how you will be catering to the needs of people properly, more and more people would want to invest in your company.

Defining the workplace environment

Although it is not mandatory, it is advisable to describe what kind of a workplace environment you wish to establish. Preferable environments are where employer-employee interactions take place and where mutual respect is observed.

Keys to Success

It is a known fact that every business depends on quite a few factors in order to be successful, but there are a few important factors upon which it depends more. These factors are the keys to success. Identifying the keys to success can help you prioritize your business better. It is advisable to pay more attention to these factors as compared to the others because in order for your business to attain fruition, it is mandatory that these elements function efficiently.

Not only do these elements give you scope to prioritize, they also help in enhancing your focus. The focus is obviously necessary in order to work efficiently. You need to identify the keys to the success of your business early on. Make sure you limit the number of elements to three or four because as you exceed this number it becomes harder to focus and this will hinder the implementation process. So, thinking of the keys to success is extremely helpful in running a business.

CHAPTER 7

STARTING YOUR BUSINESS

It may be exciting to start your own business and be on your own, but never do so without being familiar with all the fundamentals and hardships that go hand in hand with a business.

Customers are top priority

Although a business plan is essential and absolutely vital in setting up a business effectively, it is not the single most important element which is sufficient for running a company. There are quite a few other factors which come into play. For instance:

- Customers: The need for having customers cannot be overstated. Customers are quite possibly the most important requirement for starting your own business. Even if you have a tremendous business plan and an innovative idea, if there is no one to buy what you are marketing, your business will fail.

- Satisfying your customers: In order to gain customers, you need to identify a particular customer need that your business will be satisfying. If your product has no specific use in a customer's life, then there is no need for them to buy it and your business will not be successful. There needs to be some market to which your product or service will contribute in order for it to be successful.

Common misconceptions about starting a business

There are quite a few misconceptions associated with starting and running your own business. These myths should be avoided as they can eventually become the cause of a number of issues.

- The "I'm my own boss" feeling: This is by far the most common mistake most businessmen make initially. Just because you own your company does not make you your own boss. You still have customers and their needs to cater to. Banks will be demanding and so will the fixed costs. You will still have to work according to other people's convenience.

- The myth of "independence": Another popular mistake among entrepreneurs is that they believe they are independent. When you do not have any debts to fulfill and when you earn for yourself, you become independent. As long as you still have a withstanding loan with banks, you are not independent.

Another important thing to remember is that running your own company does not always entail positivity and success. Sometimes, if the business fails or if the market goes down, there are massive downsides to having your own company. Not being able to clear the loans to banks or being unable to pay your employees due to lack of money are possibilities that you may have to face in the event of a failure. Running your own company is a huge risk because it can go either way.

Different types of business plans- simple plans for startups

Most entrepreneurs, business advisors, potential investors and bankers believe that when a person is starting a business he or she should make an elaborate business plan. This, however, is not true. When you are just starting up, it is sufficient to devise a simple plan. You could always make it more elaborate and expand it as your business progresses. While submitting your plan to bankers or investors, make sure it is elaborate so that they fully understand what your company is about. Do not make it lengthy, but include every detail.

Do not let any factor like this book or any online tutorial make you devise a plan that is more elaborate than required. At the end of it all, you are the best judge of your plan. As long as your plan does what it is supposed to-organize, prioritize and land you investors-it is sufficient. Not every plan is the same, not every business needs the same level of detail.

For instance, imagine a woman making gifts for different occasions at home. She has created a page on Facebook where she is marketing the gifts that she makes in order to sell. But if she were to build a business plan, she would be able to step away from her regular flow of working and identify ways to improve business and develop the business. When she is planning, she will be able to understand her business better. She would know what it is that she wants and also understand what her customers expect from her. She could then begin to optimize the business, according to those needs. She will be able to benefit if she develops a simple task for sales and expenses. It will give her an idea on how she can use the resources that she has. She does not have to create a detailed balance sheet or cash flow statement, but a simple plan that will help her business flourish.

This does not mean that all start – ups are simple. Most of them need to have a separate plan for the development of their products, packaging, signing agreements with retail offices, equipment and machinery and also for setting up a website for their company. It is only that the company will l be able to make sales. If you are wealthy to finance your company for yourself, you do not have to meet banks and investors for loans. It is for such meetings that you will have to come up with an extensive plan. But whether or not you have the investment, you have to create a plan that meets the expectations.

The most important thing to remember while creating your business plan is to identify and meet your real business needs. You will need to create a brilliant plan which is still in the test phase when you are discussing it with a potential partner or a team member. You can add the basic aspects of sales and also make projections for the future on the profits and losses of your company. If you add business numbers, you will be able to create a bigger impact.

The ultimate choice of your plan should not be based on the stage of your business, but on the type of the business, the financing requirements and the ultimate objective. Below are a few indicators for the level of the plan that you will need to prepare:

1. It is common that for simpler businesses, the plan is always in the owner's head. But it is best to have every employee identify a certain plan since it gives them the idea of how they want their company to function. A person running a business single handedly can identify a plan when he PENS it down. This is a very useful process.

2. When the number of people increases the level of your plan multiplies. You will have to communicate goals, values and also detail every aspect of implementing the plan.

3. The minute you have potential partners involved, you will have to provide a lot of information. You will have to describe the history of your company and minute details of your product. Considering the above example. If the girl wanted to create a plan and involve an external partner, she would have to identify topics that added value to her plan and also helped support the decisions she made for the company. You have to provide a great amount of background information.

4. When you are in the phase of discussion, you can write

down what you want to tell people about your company. Tell them why you started the company and also identify what the keys to success for you are. Explain to them the basic strategies that you will be undertaking for the same. You have to check how well this plan covers your business idea.

5. Do you think your company can survive without a sales and an expense forecast? At times, the owner of the business, if it is a small business, keeps the numbers in his head. However, you can identify tools that will help you and will save a lot of time. This is why it is essential that you plan.

6. Do you have a clear idea of your market? Ave you conducted a thorough market analysis to identify if you are giving yourself a good opportunity? Do you know if your customers want what you are selling? Are you serving their needs? You will have to cover these areas while planning.

7. Are you a company that sells on credit? Do you want to sell businesses? If you do, you will have to sell on credit. You will need to create a separate system that will help you identify if there are any customers who owe you money and also how you can manage those customers. You will have to make a sale and also ensure that you earn your money. For this, you need a very sophisticated plan.

8. Do you ensure that you do your taxes on a cash basis? If you are unsure of the same, you have a small business and you provide taxes on a cash basis. This helps you plan your business easily. You only have to worry about how much cash goes into taxes. Bigger companies have a tough job here. They have to identify the different taxes that they have to pay and also identify the taxes on the expenses that they have incurred. They will need

to create an extensive business plan to identify these aspects of the plan.

9. When you approach banks and other financial institutions, you have to provide a good detail of your personal worth and also the collaterals that go into giving you your financial position. There are some banks that accept the superficial business plan when they have identified that your collaterals look good. There are some banks that would like to see your estimated projections as well. Banks will not lend money on a business plan alone, but it does hold value!

10. There are times when you begin to approach a potential investor. These investors will look into the minute details of your plan. Investors will require your plan to have a proof! They do not just look for better plans. They will have to see the analysis that you have covered about the market and also understand your management. They will have to see robust financial projections! There are times when investors have backed companies without a plan, but that is not going to lead them a great way.

No matter what anybody says, your business needs to have a plan at its initial stages. You will have to create the plan in your head to be able to tell anybody about it if you are ever asked. Before you purchase any machinery or equipment for your company, you have to create a plan to see if you can cover your investment.

Identify and Understand the Risks

You might be an entrepreneur and would have spent time with other entrepreneurs. You want to create the business that you have always dreamed of. You want to make it work! But there are hundreds and thousands of businesses that have taken more money than they could ever return. They have dug themselves into a deep, black hole and find themselves unable to get out of it. There are two important risks that you have to consider when you are beginning your business. These risks affect every kind of business.

- Product businesses need MORE INVESTMENT when compared to service businesses. This is a major factor that needs to be considered.

- When you start a business without capital, which is called Bootstrapping. You are creating a harder path for yourself if you are a product business!

CHAPTER 8

BENEFITS AND LIMITATIONS OF SWOT ANALYSIS

What is S.W.O.T Analysis

- Strengths – The advantages
- Weaknesses – The disadvantages
- Opportunities - External interesting options
- Threats – External movements which may cause a problem

S.W.O.T analysis will prepare you thoroughly to dive into the process of business planning which would eventually result into an effective business venture. Such planning is ready to function and is ready to effectively face problems. It is best to perform S.W.O.T analysis at the early stages of your business development.

Benefits

The biggest advantage of S.W.O.T analysis is the fact that it has no or very little cost involved. Any complex situation or an otherwise tedious scenario can also be looked at using S.W.O.T analysis. Of course, another really important advantage of this analysis is that it brings into focus all the crucial aspects of a business venture. Using S.W.O.T can reveal the following:

- Go deeper into understanding your business better
- Do not shy away from your weaknesses rather address them

- Be prepared for the threats and know the plan to mitigate them
- Take advantage and capitalize on opportunities
- Enhance your skill and take advantage of your strengths

Limitations of S.W.O.T analysis

S.W.O.T analysis is a starting point of making a business plan but also it is one of the many stages of planning process. S.W.O.T analysis only covers issues that can definitely be considered as strength, weakness, opportunity or threat; it is actually difficult to address uncertain factors.

Following are the limitations of S.W.O.T analysis:

- Does not provide an insight to prioritize issues
- Does not provide solutions
- Can lead to the generation of many ideas, but does not pinpoint to the most suitable one.
- Does not always provide useful information

What is P.E.S.T Analysis?

P.E.S.T helps in developing an analysis of the external factors, especially while conducting a market survey or research. These factors are:

- Politics – Global issues, policy regulations, laws or other scenarios which may affect your business either now or in the coming future.
- Economic – Stock market, consumer interests and trends, interest etc.
- Social – Any major events, lifestyle variations, ethics, media trends etc.
- Technological – Innovations, developments, resources, research and other such global communications.

S.W.O.T Analysis v/s P.E.S.T Analysis

Both S.W.O.T and P.E.S.T are the tools that help will you jot down strategically all the important aspects that your business planning will need. Both of them are extensively used to formulate and expand a business plan or any other project plan. With the help of these methods you can analyze thoroughly both internal and external factors that may affect your business. However, there are some major distinctions between the two and knowing this difference will only help the most appropriate usage of the two.

CHAPTER 9

SELL YOUR IDEA, APPROPRIATELY

At around this time would be ideal to explain your company, the strategy that underlies it and the story behind it. You also need to explain the competitive edge that your company will have over the other participants in the industry.

By now, you probably would have realized that there is no set way to develop a business plan, i.e. there is no "logical method" to follow. There is no sequence as such that you can emulate in order to create your plan. For instance, you had a brief glance at the market numbers while doing the initial analysis. You will have to look into these numbers in more detail when you analyze the market itself. These numbers will probably come up again when you analyze the entire industry that you will be contributing to. Similar to the market numbers, there are quite a few components of a business plan that you may have to revisit numerous times as you progress with your plan.

Information about your company

As mentioned earlier in this book, it is advisable to have a chapter in your business plan solely dedicated to your company. This chapter is generally placed right after the Executive Summary. If the plan is meant to be internal, i.e. if it is used only for your reference, then this topic need not be included because you are well aware of your own company. However, if this plan is to be submitted to potential investors and bankers, it needs to be included.

Summary Paragraph

It is a good practice to include a summary about your company at the beginning of the chapter on your company. You can exclude all the minute details in this summary. Try making it as short as possible so that it can make for good reading. Do not forget to mention the essentials such as the name of the company, what market it contributes to and how it caters to its customer's needs. Also include how long your company has been around for.

Legal Entity ownership

Dedicate around a paragraph to this topic. In this paragraph, you are expected to explain the ownership of the company and its legal establishment. As we know, there are many types of companies such as partnerships, corporations, sole proprietorships, etc. This part of your plan will clarify what type of company you are heading. Ownership implies that you need to explain who owns the company. If it is a partnership, you need to mention the number of owners and in what proportion they own it. You will also need to specify whether your company is a public or private entity.

Most of the small scale businesses, especially service businesses are sole proprietor businesses (only one owner). A minority of them are legal partnerships. Professional service businesses such as law firms, consulting firms and accounting firms are majorly partnerships. If you are in doubt about what type of a company you should establish, approach a business attorney.

Amenities and locations

This portion of your plan is to describe the various offices and locations of your company. Also explain the lease arrangements that you have on each of the buildings.

If you are a service business, then your company will not have manufacturing plants and factories. However, you might have other services such as call centers, internet services and other office facilities. You will be expected to explain all this in this paragraph.

The situation is different if you had a retail store. For a retail store, the location is vital. You will need to describe the location, parking facilities and traffic patterns.

However, if your company is into manufacturing, then you will be expected to describe the plants and factories that are meant for production, assembly and other purposes. Also describe the method of transportation of goods, if any.

So, depending on the purpose of your plan and the type of company you run, you may or may not want to include details about other facilities.

Be strategic

Probably one of the most important advantages of developing a business plan is that it allows you to think in depth about your own company. This was already discussed earlier as the mini plan with the mission statement and keys to success.

Competitive Edge

You need to know the competitive edge that your company has over other companies in the same industry. You need to be aware of what characterizes your company and makes it stand out above the rest. There needs to be some reason why customers will wish to choose your product over the products of the other companies. You also need to be able to maintain your company at the top level for a very long time for it to be successful. Having patented technology and higher market shares are important in order to have a competitive edge over other companies.

The most contributing factor or rather the most recognizable type of competitive edges arise from having proprietary technology. If your company possesses patents or self-developed algorithms, there is a massive competitive edge that it will receive. For service businesses, however, the edges may arise from simpler factors such as having toll free numbers.

Baseline Numbers

This part is dedicated to establishing the starting number for your company (the cash flow and balance sheet). In case, your company has been running for some time now, the starting (baseline) numbers that you will establish now will be the last balance from the past.

Past performances of previously established companies

If you are running a company that has been around for a while, you will also have to include a summary of the company's history in the plan. Details like financial results of the past will be expected by the investors and bankers and this is the part of the plan where you will mention them.

In case of a change in sales and profits (be it an increase or a decrease), you will have to explain why it has happened. You may also include certain big moments for your company over the past few years such as new services, new locations or new partners. Basically, this segment of the plan covers the company's history right from the founding till the present day and it includes all the major events and changes that your company has experienced.

However, do not make it too detailed such that it becomes like a history lesson for the reader of the plan. You must not bore the reader by including irrelevant or insignificant details about your company's history. You have to mention only those events or changes which the reader will require to understand the background of your company.

Initial costs for startup companies

The initial portion of any startup table estimates the start-up expenses. You first need to familiarize yourself with the differences between expenses and assets. This is extremely important and it is advisable to first fully understand it and then continue. To be precise, start-up expenses are the costs incurred before the implementation of the plan. Any expenses that are incurred after the implementation has begun, they belong on the profit and loss table.

Many common start-up expenses are included in this table like stationery costs, advertising costs and legal costs. Another popular expense is the costs incurred in purchasing the equipment for offices such as computers and telephones. It makes sense to categorize these as assets, but they are expensed because that reduces the taxable income and so the government allows these items to be classified as expenses rather than assets.

Confusions arise when it comes to product development expenses. Some people prefer to make them assets when they are actually to be treated as expenses. Although most people would want them to be assets that can develop in the future, they are treated as expenses when it comes to levying taxes.

Initial assets

To reiterate, make sure you know exactly what the differences between assets and expenses are. Assets are possessions of the company (goods and documents) that have a transferable value. They make the company's balance sheet more reputable. However, given the choice between classifying a certain item as an expense or an asset, most people choose to brand it as an expense so that they can reduce the amount of taxable income because the expenses are directly deducted from the income of the company.

The cash that you start your company ultimately comes from the amount you raise through loans and investments. When you find that you need more money, you will have to raise more money through loans or investments. When you increase the amount of money that you need, you will have to increase the cash that you have. For instance, when you begin your company, you may have a starting balance of $50,000 which includes both your loans and the investments. When you verify your start up assets and expenses, you have a total amount of $50, 000 which proves that your calculation is balanced. But if you had raised $1, 00, 000 through loans and investments and only specified that you had $50, 000 as your start up assets and expenses, you would lose out on the $50, 000 since that is accounted as funding. Instead, you can add that amount to your starting cash, or capital, which will increase the value of your assets.

There is another difference that you need to be very clear about. The money that you want to have in your bank account at the start-up phase is different from the money that has been raised to start the business. The money that has been raised needs to equal the amount spent on expenses and procuring assets. In fact, the money at start-up is actually an asset. Increasing the money raised implies that you need to increase the start-up expenses and this is generally done by increasing the starting cash. This money is used to fund start-up expenses as well as start-up assets.

CHAPTER 10

DESCRIBE WHAT YOU SELL!

This is the most important step to your plan. You always send your plan out to external readers – bankers, investors – to ensure that they are impressed by your company. You have to describe to them the products and services that your company sells!

This section of your plan is the most important! It includes a lot of details like the prices, the material used and certain bills that have been incurred by you while procuring material. This is often a text based section of your business plan. It is mentioned right before the market analysis, but after the description of your company.

Begin with a summary

Like every other section of your business plan, this must also have an opening paragraph that describes what the rest of the section. This paragraph can be used effectively while creating your summary memos and loan application. You can use it to support your company while approaching an investor or a bank for a loan. You might find that a person reading your plan will skip the details when he has found your summary paragraph effective. This can be a paragraph that covers every aspect of your company. To do justice to this section, you have to identify what you are selling and to whom.

Write a detailed description

The previous aspect covers only the summary of the products. You will have to provide details to every section of your product in this section. You will have to describe the products and services that you are selling. You will have to cover the main aspects of your business, including how the product or service benefits your customers. You will have to also mention whether the customer needs the product or not.

You do not have to include every product or service that you are providing in the list, but you will have to include the most important details. It is a good idea to put yourself in your customer's shoes and see how the products and services you are offering benefit them. It is best if you consider them over your idea of a business. You will have to see how you will deliver the products and services to your customer. While planning, you might find a whole new set of ideas that you can use!

You will have to describe your products in detail and also cover every type of customer that you are targeting. On your way, you might find that there is more that you can do! You can generate a bunch of new ideas this way!

Compare your company with your competitors

This part of your plan must be used elaborately by you. You will have to think of it from the perspective of your clients. You have to see what other options a customer has in the market and design this analysis. There is a separate section on market analysis that covers every aspect of your competitors and your products. You will identify the strengths and the weaknesses and see how you are better when compared to your competitors.

In this section, you will have to discuss the product lines that you offer and see how the retail offerings from various companies are. You will have to compare a retail market offer with the next. For example, if you have a store that is located in the market, you might be a company dealing with jewelry. You may be a company that has a mid – range in prices, but the people who have purchased at your store know that the quality is brilliant! You may have a shop that caters to different hobbies and passions. Your shop may have a wide range of guitars and other instruments that you can use to generate business!

In simple words, you will have to discuss your position in the market. You will have to see why people buy from your business instead of the others who are in the same line of business. What is it about your products that attract the customers? You will have to identify specific benefits and features. Describe the important competitive factors instead of the general factors of your products.

Fulfillment and Sourcing

This section deals with product sourcing and the cost that goes into fulfilling your service. You will need your manufacturers and assemblers to provide you with the list of different costs incurred by the company and the overhead cost as well. This is with respect to manufacturing companies. If you own a servicing company, you will have to identify the cost that has been incurred by your company while fulfilling obligations.

For instance, assume that you own a manufacturing company. Sourcing is an important factor for your company. You will have vendors who will determine the standard costs that you will incur and will hold the key to your operational expenses. You will have to analyze the standard costs and also identify the services that you will have to purchase to enhance the manufacturing of your products. Identify the strengths and the weaknesses.

Manufacturing companies always have plenty of information when it comes to resource planning and sourcing material for the manufacture of products. This is essential for the plans that you will be sharing with bankers and investors or when you are evaluating your business. This helps you have additional documentation which you can attach when signing contracts with suppliers or assessing bills and for any other information.

There are materials that are vital for the manufacturing of products in your company. For this you will have to identify secondary sources and other alternative sources. You will have to work on maintaining a healthy relationship with these sources in order to fall back on them when you are in need. This will help you identify the benefit of your sourcing strategy.

Sourcing and fulfillment is not only for product based companies, but also for different industries. You will need to source and also fulfill the obligations to your customers if you are a financial company or a graphic design company. You will have to source professionals who will be able to deliver products based on the needs of your customers.

Mention the future products

You will have to identify the products that you would want to sell in the future. You have to identify if you have a long – term strategy in place for your products. Have you established a relationship between the different market segments, the demand and needs and the products that you develop?

What you include in this section depends on the nature of your plan. You may have investors who are always eager to know what you would want to do in the future. They are keen to analyze the future prospects of your company. But there are banks to consider too! They do not provide loans for the hopes of future products. If you are writing a plan for a loan application, you do not have to stress too much on this section. You can simply list out the products that you would like to develop in the future.

You will have to deal with the aspect of confidentiality. When you list out new products or future products in your plan, you have to make sure that nobody steals those ideas and calls them their own for their company. You have to ensure that the people who receive copies of your plan are trustworthy and will work towards the benefit of the company. You can also make the recipients sign a non – disclosure agreement!

A review on sales

It is a great idea to include specific items of sale and also see what collaterals you can include to enhance your business plan. If you have a company that deals with the passions and hobbies of people you can use the different instruments that you have or the model airplanes that you have as collateral. You can show your investors and partners what it is about your shop that attracts people the way bees are attracted towards honey. You must explain to them the feel and view of your company.

It is always a good idea to discuss your current situation with your investors and partners. It is even better to provide them with your future plans! When you are writing a review on your sales, it is best to provide the current image of your company along with the services provided by your company. You can also talk about how you are working towards cutting costs!

CHAPTER 11

DEFINE YOUR TARGET AUDIENCE

Conduct a research on the potential consumer audience for your product/ services in order to not confuse in this big vast world, where it is extremely important to know otherwise you will be lost and your objectives might not take you where you actually see your business project implanted.

Depending on the kind of business you are venturing into - if it is online then obviously the pool of people could be in millions or if it is a retail store or client service it could be in thousands. It also depends on the demography of your business. The demographic distribution of population in a big city is very different from that of a small town.

It is important to know your demographic reach. It is essential that you scale down your research to the most granular detail and identify the demographic distribution of the kind of population you would reach out to. This kind of thorough research will attract more investors and stakeholders; it will also make it much easier for you to create a great marketing plan.

Go deeper with your research, even it means going back and forth and re looking at your values, goals, objectives or maybe you already have this understanding but it is extremely important to put it down. Identification of your audience is one of the most critical aspects in your planning process.

Ask questions:

- What is my business project going to bring to the market?

- What is the unique quality about it?

- What might appeal to people?

- Do not guess. Though it is a shortcut, it will not yield fruitful results

- On defining the target audience, do the following:

- Describe the most granular details about your target audience

- Explain and showcase how your business plan actually will impact the lives of our target audience

- Define the intention and motivation

- Explain how your business will roll out

- Explain the changes that the execution of your business plan will bring about

- Your vision and mission

Break - even analysis

It is a key aspect of any good business plan. It sounds complicated, but it is not really rocket science. If put in a very basic language, breakeven means to analyze - how many hours/expense/ units of stuff etc it will take to cover the costs.

You will need the following information:

- Fixed costs per month

- Variable costs per unit

- Average price per unit

Break-Even Analysis: Fixed Costs

Fixed costs are the ones that do not change frequently like your monthly rent or salary. These are costs that do not vary up or down the scale no matter how many products or units you sell. If you are a start, it is best not to rely on guesswork when estimating your costs. It is important to perform a complete and thorough research on every cost related aspect before you lay down the budgets and costing.

Break-Even Analysis: Variable Costs

Variable costs are the ones that keep varying depending on the sale and other external scenarios. Things like inventory, shipping costs, commissions, etc cannot remain fixed.

Break-Even Analysis: Pricing

This is the most critical and without a doubt the trickiest of all the aspects. Once you know and have absolute clarity on the above two you can now go ahead and fix a price. For that you also need to know the current market price of the product by your competitors so that you do not end up setting up an undervalued price for your product/service etc.

Break-Even Analysis: The Formula

Once your analysis is done, all you need to do is plug everything into this formula, and there you go, your complete information:

BEQ = Fixed costs / (Average price per unit – average cost per unit)

Benefits and Limitations of break – even analysis

When making a business it is extremely important that you have a clear understanding of your finances. Keep them in check and do a thorough assessment. Break - even analysis is the best tool to propel this and the best part about this tool is its simplicity and ease. It is used to understand and construct a helpful mechanism where the whole management can understand the relationship between cost-volume- profit and the challenges associated with it.

Make v/s Buy:

The cost-volume- profit analysis propels in making a judgment call of whether to buy or manufacture products on your own. If this analysis shows an indication that highlights that the cost of internally manufacturing much lesser than what would be paid to the external vendor then a call needs to be taken that is most appropriate. 2. Production planning:

Cost control:

The cost-volume- profit analysis can be used as a cost control parameter. It can be used to immediately indicate any steep rise in the costs which otherwise would have gone unnoticed.

Financial structure:

It is important to understand this structure in order to plan things forward. Break - even analyses provides the understanding of how profit functions with respect to output. A very important insight indeed!

Conditions of uncertainty:

With the help of break - even analysis it becomes possible to demystify the whole decision making process. This clarity comes from the fact that this analysis provides immense clarity to the whole process.

Limitations:

- This analysis does not show distinctions between the different components of costs and also fails to properly demarcate fixed cost from variable cost.

- In case where company's sale of products is really high in that case it very difficult to keep a track of the profit scale.

- Since the break - even relationship represents only short term analysis; there is a high probability that it becomes redundant real soon.

- The relations that are indicated in break even analysis do not penetrate into different set of operations

- If there are erratic changes within the organization that are not very cohesive with the existing market then there is a high chance that break - even analysis cannot be relied upon.

CHAPTER 12

MANAGEMENT TEAM

The management team of your company is an extremely important entity! It is like a limb of your body. While hiring the members for your management team, you will have to ensure that they are capable of handling the functions of your company and also see if they are able to trust each other and work as a team. It is the trust factor that decides whether your company flourishes or not!

What kind of people do you need?

Consider this small example! It is a beautiful day outside. There are people bustling around in your company going about their business. Looking at the wondrous atmosphere, you decide to order Chinese for lunch today!

The accountant has tallied all the accounts for your financial year. She is joyous and has just stepped out of her office. She is walking towards the administrator's room when she sees everybody gathered around the reception. Looking at the people around, she decides to start a discussion about her footwear. She tells everybody that they should enjoy her footwear since she is wearing her favorite pair! Everybody laughs but on taking a closer look find the footwear beautiful.

The head of the IT department has called everybody's attention to the accountant's hair. He states that her hair reminds him of noodles. Everybody begins to laugh. They continue to chat away while enjoying their lunch. They start making jokes on every person in the room and have a gala time.

The marketing head has just walked out of her room and has joined the discussion. She starts telling everybody about the Zumba dance class that she has joined. She turns the music on and performs a few steps! The other employees are hooting and cheering her on.

The auditing manager has emerged from her colorful office and announces to the room that there is a new couch in her office and asks everybody to come there for lunch instead of having to stand and eat.

The entire office is happy. Every person is spreading happiness and has never had a problem communicating with each other. They are able to communicate well to their customers as well. The age gap between the employees does not cause any problems between the employees. These people like each other and are able to work very well with each other.

Now imagine how your company was a few years ago! You would have been worried sick about how to set up your company. Your accountant would be worried about how much money is in the company, the marketing head and the sales manager were worried about how they can publicize their products to ensure greater sales. These people, including you, were only able to manage their jobs without knowing if that job was what they wanted to do.

If you had jumped right into planning on how to make the people work based on their curriculum vitae you would find that your company does not meet your goals of profit. You can only have your company at its best when your employees work together and gel together. If you have a very good environment at work, you can ensure that the products and services that you have work wonders in the market!

CHAPTER 13

BE FAMILIAR WITH YOUR BUSINESS

In addition to everything you will be mentioning in your business plan you will also have to explain the type of business you are in. As in, explaining what your company does will not be enough. You will also have to describe the workplace environment among other things.

If your plan is being submitted to bankers or potential investors you will be expected to explain the state of your company and also the nature of your business. Whether or not your company is blooming is another important detail that you will have to specify in your plan.

No matter what type of business you run, be it a service business or a retailer business, you need to have a part of your plan dedicated to Industry Analysis which explains the following:

- Industry Participants.
- Distribution Patterns.
- Competition.

Let us explore these topics in greater detail.

Industry Analysis

In this chapter, we look to emphasize on the massive impact that the internet has had on Business Information. Procuring information on business is not a problem anymore as most people know how to use the internet to gain information. Ever since the information explosion in the 1990's, gathering information has become child's play. However, there still exists the problem of sorting the information.

There are websites out there for almost everything. Any help that you may need in making your business plan can be sought out online. Marketing strategies, demographics, advertising strategies and many other factors that are vital to running a business can all be learned about on the internet. At the end of the chapter are listed certain references in case you really need them.

Industry Participants

An essential component in describing the type of business you are in is the nature of the participants in that industry. This is important as there are many variations to the number of participants. For instance, there are some businesses which have only a few big companies as participants all over the world. However, there are a few generic businesses which involve tens of thousands of participants all around the world

This clearly can make a huge difference to both your business and business plan. Industries like dry cleaners and restaurants are what is known as pulverized industries because there are so many participants involved worldwide. On the other hand, the fast food business is different. Although it may seem to be a pulverized industry, there are a few big companies across the world, which have their numerous outlets.

There is a term known as consolidation when it comes to industries. Economists define this term as the phase during which certain participants become large and outshine the other smaller participants. These smaller participants eventually disappear. For instance, when we consider the hotel industry, there a few big names that are known all across the world and some smaller hotels those remain on a national or regional level. This can be seen in any industry for that matter.

Identify the patterns of distribution

When you are clear about the industry you are in, you will have to also identify how the distribution of products works in the industry. You will have to see whether the products and services you provide can be distributed through retailers in different regions. For instance, if you are a company that designs and manufactures clothes, you will need to find an outlet which will help you sell the clothes. This is the same for electronic products, magazines and automobiles. You have to see whether you can support your own sales or whether you have to work with representatives who will help with the sales of your products and services.

There are some products that are always sold through retail stores. There are other products that are purchased by the distributors from the manufacturers and sold in the market. There are other times when the manufacturer himself sells the products to the customers. There are times when the manufacturer directly communicates with the consumer to sell his products. For instance, he could start a campaign on the internet. The page he creates for this can be visited by any person interested in the products!

There are different categories of products that can be distributed through different means. You can have door – to – door sales and sell vacuum cleaners and encyclopedias. You can also sell these by advertising through radio and television. They can then be sold directly by the manufacturer.

There are many products that can be distributed through direct business. The long term contracts that exist between car manufacturers and the suppliers of their parts and materials are a classic example. Some companies use representatives and agents to distribute their products. The recent advancements in technology help in a wide spread distribution of products. The internet helps you access books that are in a different country entirely.

This section is not required for some services that are available in the market. If you have a company that is in the restaurant business, or an architect or any other service that does not involve distribution of products you can delete this topic. You do not necessarily have to advertise the services that you provide or walk to the market to sell the services. However, for a few services you can identify the distribution patterns. If you are a cable service provider, you can describe the areas where you distribute your services and also talk about any physical infrastructure that the customer might require.

Identify the competition

You will have to conduct research to understand the competition in the market. Here you will have to describe the industry and also the type of business you are in. Explain why the customers always choose one service provider over the next. Identify the strengths and weaknesses of the industry.

What are the key aspects of success? What are the factors of the products that make the most difference when it comes to sales? The competition depends on reputation and trend and different aspects of the market. The selling channels make the most difference when it comes to identifying different aspects of competition.

In the food industry, the competition always depends on the perception that people have on the market. A chef is hired in an instant if he is from Cordon Bleu. It is always about the reputation and the trend.

The nature of competition depends on word of mouth in quite a few professional services. Why does a person hire a wedding planner instead of organizing their own wedding? Why would a person go to Starbucks instead of drinking coffee at a local coffee house? Why would they approach one doctor instead of the other? This is because of the nature of competition.

Identify your main competitors!

This step is highly essential! You will have to list your main competitors in the market. If you are a company dealing with selling gold, you will have to see how the other companies selling gold are performing and identify your main competition from that list. You will then have to identify why those competitors have performed well in the areas you are weak in. Assess their strengths and their weaknesses. Identify the different technology they use and how it benefits their company. Also analyze why they pose a threat to your company. You can conduct a thorough S.W.O.T analysis on the same.

Discover Information

The internet is your best friend here! You find just about anything on the internet. You will know that there is enough help available for you when it comes to business information and entrepreneurial help. You have to start on the Internet. There are numerous market research firms that have published their study on the internet. They publish truckloads of information on different industries which will help you analyze the state of your company if you do choose to expand. There are certain companies that have provided their statistics on the internet which will help you identify if that company is in fact a competitor to you. There are numerous laws that state that companies have to provide their financial records on the internet. These laws are your arsenal of weapons! You can procure information on different companies because of the existence of such laws. You can download the information from the websites onto your computer through certain databases. You can find statistical and accounting abstracts available on the internet which provides you with a base for conducting your research.

If you are not a person who is savvy with the technology, it is best for you to learn! You have to give yourself the facility of free internet access. Get yourself a modem and learn how to access and browse through the internet. You will be able to communicate with people who live across the globe, learn from them and also identify different strategies together. You can gain advice from people who have been in the field for over a decade. The internet provides you with a lot of facilities for which you find no other substitute. It is best for you to learn the ways of the internet to flourish!

You might prefer to use the local library as an alternative to the Internet. But what you forget is that the internet has the latest updates. You can always find documented versions of the laws and publications provided by many companies and industries. You can also find information about your government!

CHAPTER 14

FINANCIAL PLANNING

The most essential, important and serious aspect of any business plan is its financial planning process. There are certain documents required for financial planning process. These statements actually show the current financial status of the company. This is also beneficial in understanding and reflecting on the measures that need to be taken to take the company where it needs to be. It also helps potential investors to determine how much money they will be interested to give.

The data and information that these financial statements contain is highly useful. This information is important to fragment the minor details of that give the exact picture of every factor that incorporates the DNA of the organization/company.

It is important that you are absolutely clear and certain about a few things before you step into seeking financing. Honestly ask yourself if you are ready for the risk of borrowing the money? Where the money is and what is it needed for? What would be the consequences?

Begin your financial plan with thorough depth and knowledge about the current status of where your organization/company stands today financially, where it will be in next five years and what has been its historical situation. Only when all this is clear, go ahead with charting out the financial targets.

You know you are on the right track when your financial statements reflect both long term and a short term objectives/targets of your business venture. The projections of your business plan should be realistic and not based on optimistic or cautious presumptions. Also, be aware that investors look out for certainty and not assumptions.

What financial plan actually shows if put in the simplest manner is to say how much money your business venture requires? It is important to be well informed about the amount of money that you need before you extend a hand for the investors. If you still do not know the amount of money that you need, do not worry, you will figure it out eventually. Do not shy away from providing a probable figure.

Remember, a lender or an investor does not want the complete details, but what he wants to see is the depth of your preparation, your vision and the clarity that you present. What they look out for is commitment; once they see that there is no way that you would be left without a good amount of funding

The consolidation of financial statements is of course very important, but other than that it is also critical that you make sure that none of these statements have any sort mistakes - calculations or spelling errors. Substandard will only reduce your chances to get the money. Ask for help from a professional if you think you lack the expertise in preparing these financial statements.

It is actually good to hire a consultant for all this work. This most often gives a more fair and unbiased output. Such an expert also keeps a check on your future projections and also advises you on whether you are on the right track or not.

You just cannot afford to make any mistakes when preparing your financial plan. So make sure that you invest a good amount of time and energy in formulating this piece of work otherwise there is a high chance that your whole business plan might come crumbling down.

There are certain must haves when preparing a financial statement. These are defying factors that help identify the success rate of your business. Here is your list of essentials when preparing a financial statement.

Income Statement

Income statement is a detailed document that gives information about the total income and the revenues that your company generates over a specific time period. What lenders and investors want to see is the profitability of your company and income statement representing that credibility, which basically proves and shows the kind of money your business is making.

Balance Sheet

It is important to have knowledge about the liabilities and assets that your company might be entailing. It is very useful information when you are trying to calculate the profits that your business has made. The balance sheet shows the exact financial position of the company at a particular given point of time. It is a highly informative document that at any cost cannot be missed.

Cash Flow statement

The understanding of cash flow statement gives an insight on the amount of money that should be spent out of the company/ organization and the amount of money that should be coming into the organization in a definite time period. A cash flow statement is a futuristic document. It gives a realistic insight into how much budget would be required to cover operational costs for both long term and short term time period. This could be anything between 3 to 5 years of timeline. It is an important tool to declare your projections.

Typical elements of financial analysis:

Budgeting

Creating a budget and setting out a planned cash flow is very important. By monitoring a cash flow it becomes easy to identify crisis situations thus avoiding last minute stress and confusion. Budgets can also be set out for income and expenditure by the business. Budget can also indicate any major investment in the capital.

Profit - loss analysis

This involves the profit - loss account setting. It is usually set on the basis of the probable future profits and losses that the business entails. Practical parts of productivity analysis are:

- operating profit (on percentage of the sale)
- gross profit (on percentage of the sale)

Solvency analysis

This element involves calculating the net current assets of a business as shown in the balance sheet (i.e. current assets - current liabilities).

Return on capital employed (ROCE)

This is a measure of the return made on all of the capital employed in the business in a given period of time.

Analyze the returns

Where a business has shareholders it is useful to analyze returns to these shareholders in terms of returns of income spent in shared capital. Financial analysis is very important in planning business. Ultimately, it is all about money and investors in a business

- Need to feel that their money is secure
- Need to see that their returns are comparable to what they can earn elsewhere
- Need to know that there are good implications of this investment.

CONCLUSION

A business plan is not merely a lengthy document that will help you procure funds. It is a thorough representation of detailed analysis, study and examination of the viability of your business idea.

Preparing your business plan in the early stages of developing your business is the best way forward. It will not only save time, but will also show you your exact market position - your strengths and weaknesses. This way you can always improve on things that you might be lacking, thus avoiding some serious mistakes.

It is very much possible that in the process of putting together your business plan, you might come across things that hadn't actually thought of, which were actually critical and important. Things like marketing budget or government regulations or some other factors that you hadn't counted in which might potentially affect your business. In putting together your plan, you will really examine your business through every lens.

One common mistake that everyone does is by not revisiting their business once made. Do not throw away or store your business plan as any other book that must be still lying in your bookshelf eating dust. It is important you keep going back to your business plan and make it your life.

As you proceed forward in your business, there will be some components that would get deleted and may be some that might get added. As your business evolves, you will know where you stand and at that time your business plan will be your single point reference.

There is no doubt that putting together a good business plan takes a tremendous amount of work. But once you have done this job, be assured to have great results.

Free Bonus Video:
Examples and Best Practices Of Business Plan Writing

Bonus Video:
https://www.youtube.com/watch?v=RoytcBiOpDI

Checkout My Other Books

http://www.amazon.com/Negotiating-Strategies-Techniques-Influencing-Negotiation-ebook/dp/B00SOK8ODI/ref=sr_1_1?s=digital-text&ie=UTF8&qid=1428982506&sr=1-1&keywords=negotiating

http://www.amazon.com/Job-Interview-Techniques-Negotiating-Persuasion-ebook/dp/B00PFFK7EE/ref=sr_1_6?s=digital-text&ie=UTF8&qid=1428982721&sr=1-6&keywords=job+interview

http://www.amazon.com/Sales-Influence-Interview-Negotiating-Persuasion-ebook/dp/B00WP84MBS/ref=sr_1_5?s=digital-text&ie=UTF8&qid=1433477607&sr=1-5&keywords=sales

Made in the USA
San Bernardino, CA
24 July 2015